Christmas Eve was here, and the snow was falling. Jenny and her parents moved to a new house in a rural area earlier in the year.

Jenny didn't believe
Santa was coming
to her house this year.
Her parents tried convincing
her that Santa visits
every house in the world.

How could Santa come?
Jenny lived in
the middle of nowhere.
She didn't even
have a chimney on her roof.
Jenny put out
milk and cookies for Santa,
even though she had her doubts.

Jenny went to bed expecting Christmas Day to be like any other day.

In the middle of the night came a loud thump on the roof. Jenny rolled over in bed and went back to sleep.

Christmas morning arrived, and Jenny walked downstairs like any other morning.

Jenny saw the Christmas Tree and underneath it was filled with presents!

How could this be?
There's no way Santa came,
but the milk and cookies
were gone!

Jenny opened her presents and received everything she wanted for Christmas. From that day forward, Jenny believed in Santa and the magic of Christmas.

The End